Beginning Fun With
Scissors

Written and compiled by Jean Warren
Illustrated by Marion Hopping Ekberg

Totline
PUBLICATIONS

Warren Publishing House
A Division of Frank Schaffer Publications
Torrance, California

Warren Publishing House would like to acknowledge the following childcare professionals for contributing some of the activities in this book: Barbara Backer, Charleston, SC and Janice Bodenstedt, Jackson, MI.

Editor: Kathleen Cubley

Contributing Editors: Gayle Bittinger, Susan Hodges, Elizabeth McKinnon

Proofreader: Kris Fulsaas

Cover Design: Brenda Mann Harrison

Interior Design & Production: Brenda Mann Harrison, Sarah Ness

Production Manager: Jo Anna Brock

Editorial Assistant: Durby Peterson

ISBN 1-57029-141-1

Printed in the United States of America
Published by Warren Publishing House
Editorial Office: P.O. Box 2250
                    Everett, WA 98203
Business Office: 23740 Hawthorne Blvd.
                    Torrance, CA 90505

20 19 18 17 16 15 14 13 12 11 10 9 8 7 6 5 4 3 2

Most children can hardly wait to get their hands on scissors.

Take advantage of this interest, because cutting with scissors is an important developmental skill that promotes fine-motor coordination and leads to the proper use of writing tools.

Using scissors seems like an easy skill to master, but there are some important steps to follow to insure successful cutting experiences. By first starting with scissor holding and manipulation techniques and then moving on to simple snipping projects, *Beginning Fun With Scissors* gives you all the hints and activities you need to help your child meet with cutting success.

Art activities are a special component of *Beginning Fun With Scissors*. The simple act of cutting is great fun for kids, but it can also produce pride and enthusiasm as your child creates his or her own art materials by snipping, clipping, and fringing with scissors.

A Word About Safety: To make sure your child's cutting adventures are safe ones, supervise your beginning cutter closely. In fact, first cutting activities are best done with your child seated at a table next to you. Be sure to discuss basic scissors safety, such as always carry scissors point-side down and pass scissors to others with the handles first. Your child should never run while holding scissors.

Last, but certainly not least, talk to your child about using scissors only on paper. You don't want a good bedsheet turned into a ghost and a younger child to end up with a new haircut!

Happy cutting!

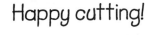

Cutting Movements

Before your child is ready to use scissors, she needs to practice using the proper cutting movements. Help your child practice finger strength and coordination by doing the movements to the following song several times.

SUNG TO: "Jimmy Crack Corn"

Open wide, squeeze them tight.
(Open fingers wide, then make a tight fist.)
Open wide, squeeze them tight.
Open wide, squeeze them tight
In the morning and at night.

Barbara Backer

Open and Shut

Show your child how the fingers open and the thumb pulls away as you cut. Several times throughout the day, help him practice this motion without scissors while you sing the following song together.

SUNG TO: "Old MacDonald"

Watch my fingers open, shut;
That's the way I cut.
Watch my fingers open, shut;
That's the way I cut.

With a snip, snip here
And a clip, clip there;
Here a snip, there a clip,
Everywhere a snip, clip.
Watch my fingers open, shut;
That's the way I cut.

Barbara Backer

Now your child is ready to practice with real scissors. Give him a pair of child-safe scissors to use to practice cutting an imaginary piece of paper. Then, hold a piece of sturdy paper, such as a large index card or similar type of paper, in both of your hands and guide it through your child's scissors as he opens and shuts them to the song.

Cutting Modeling Dough

Cutting dough is a great way for your child to build the strength and skills necessary for successful paper cutting. Show your child how to use a rolling pin to flatten pieces of dough. Help her use scissors to cut skinny "snakes" from the dough, and then thicker ones. Set out tongue depressors or plastic knives to give your child another kind of cutting experience.

After cutting practice is over, let your child use the dough snakes to build structures or arrange them to make designs.

Snipping Fringe

Give your child a pair of scissors and let her begin the cutting motions. While your child cuts, move a piece of paper from right to left so she is snipping fringe along the paper's edge.

After several pieces of paper have been fringed, show your child how to hold the paper in one hand and move it through the scissors while snipping fringe.

Give her several colors of paper to fringe. Cut the fringe off of the papers and let her use it in art projects. Green fringe can be made into grass, yellow fringe can be glued around a paper plate to make a sun, and almost any color fringe can be used for hair.

Snipping Strips

For a great beginning cutting activity, give your child 1/2-inch-wide strips of paper to snip into small squares. After this activity is mastered, give him similar strips with thick lines drawn across them and have him practice cutting on the lines. Over a period of days, provide wider strips of paper and, eventually, draw wavy lines on the strips.

Hint: To help your child remember to move the paper through the scissors and not to turn and move the scissors to cut the paper, have him pretend the elbow of his "cutting arm" is attached to the table with glue.

Things to Make With Strip Scraps

Snipping paper strips is great for developing cutting skills and a fun way for your child to make her own art materials. Whenever your child is snipping strips, provide her with a paper sack to place the scraps in. Encourage your child to make use of the scraps in art projects such as the ones below.

• Your child can dump out all of her scraps and find those that are shaped like squares. Draw a house or building shape on a piece of construction paper and let your child glue her square shapes on to make windows.

• Encourage your child to use her scraps to make colorful mosaic pictures. Draw a large square frame on a piece of construction paper, and let her glue individual paper scraps inside the frame to create the mosaic.

• Draw a picture of a tree or a birthday cake and let your child glue on colorful square and rectangle scraps to make presents.

Hint: To add variety to scrap activities, give your child strips cut from different types of paper, such as wrapping paper, wallpaper, stationery, old greeting cards, colored construction paper, and metallic paper. Let her snip the strips and then use them to make leaves on trees, scales on fish, petals on flowers, snowflakes in the air, and so on.

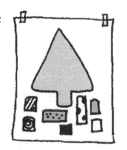

Snipping Straws and Cutting Corners

Set out some plastic straws and let your child snip them into pieces. Now give him a piece of paper. Show him how to snip the corners off of the paper. Point out how more corners appear as he cuts. Let your child cut off these new corners, too.

Use a hole punch to punch holes in the bigger corner snips. Wrap tape around the end of a piece of yarn to make a threading needle. Let your child alternate stringing straw pieces and corners to make a necklace or bracelet.

Dinosaur Lashes

For this fun cutting activity, draw lines three-quarters of the way across two 1-inch-by-3-inch pieces of paper. Give the pieces of paper to your child and let her cut the paper just to the end of each line. Now show her how to curl the paper along the cut edge with a pencil to make large eyelashes. Let her hold the lashes up to her eyes or attach them to a drawing of a dinosaur face.

Royal Crowns

Paper crowns provide a great opportunity for cutting practice. Cut several 4- by 20-inch paper headbands for your child. Encourage him to snip along the top edge of the crown to make a fringed or pointed pattern. Let your child make different types of cuts on several crowns, then help him decorate a crown with felt tip markers, rubber stamps, or stickers. Tape the completed crowns to fit around your child's head. Let him set up a "royal tea party" where all the guests wear crowns.

"Cutting" Garden

Give your child several paper baking cups in assorted colors.
Let her snip the cups from the outside edge inward, then flatten them to form flowers. Help her glue the flowers across the
middle of a piece of construction paper. Cut strips from a piece
of green construction paper to make stems. Have your child
snip another green strip of construction paper into small
squares. Let her glue on the stems, and then help her turn the
squares sideways so they resemble diamond shapes. Let her fin-
ish her garden by gluing the diamond shapes to the stems to
make leaves.

Holiday Scissor Activities

Turn busy holiday times into cutting opportunities for your child. Along with practicing cutting, your child will be creating a holiday decoration or present. Try the following ideas throughout the year.

Halloween—Let your child cut the corners from pieces of black paper to make triangles and snip strips to make squares. Give your child a paper plate and let her color it orange. Then draw a jack-o'-lantern smile (with no teeth) on the paper plate and let your child glue on squares for teeth and triangles for eyes and a nose.

Thanksgiving—Give your child strips of yellow, red, and orange construction paper. Let him snip the strips into pieces. Set out  pieces of brown construction paper and some glue and let your child glue the snipped pieces onto the brown paper to make Thanksgiving placemats. Cover the placemats with clear self-stick paper to make them more durable.

Christmas—Fold a piece of green construction paper in half lengthwise and cut it into a triangle. Starting at one end of the paper, draw equally spaced lines from the open edge halfway across the paper toward the fold. Starting from the open edges, let your child cut the paper just to the end of each line. Then have her open the paper and decorate her "tree" with circle sticker "ornaments."

Hanukkah—Give your child several small, square pieces of paper. Let him cut them in half diagonally. Then show him how to place one triangle point side down and the other on top of it point side up to make a Star of David.

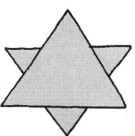

Valentine's Day—Give your child strips of red and pink paper to snip into small pieces. Let her spread glue on a heart shape and decorate it with the construction paper pieces to make a valentine.

Easter—Hold short pieces of colored yarn taut for your child to snip in half. Let him decorate paper egg shapes by gluing on the yarn pieces.

Fourth of July—Hold a piece of white paper taut and let your child cut it into strips. Set out red and blue paper, glue, and some star stickers and help her make "stars and stripes" designs.

Parent resources from Totline® Publications

the most trusted name in early learning resource books

Learning Everywhere

Children can learn all around the house and everywhere they go. Let the easy-to-follow directions in these books point the way to using ordinary materials for family fun and learning about language, art, science, math, problem solving, self-esteem, and more!

128 pp. each • For ages 2–5

A Year of Fun

Are you interested in laying a strong foundation for later learning for your children? Then you want *A Year of Fun*. Each of these books is a great resource for age-appropriate activities, child development, and practical parenting advice.

32 pp. each

Just for Babies, Just for One's, Just for Two's, Just for Three's, Just for Four's, Just for Five's

Totline® Books are available at parent & teacher stores.